Published in 2005 by
Stewart, Tabori & Chang
An imprint of Harry N. Abrams, Inc.

Text copyright ©2005 Sara Neumeier

Photographs copyright ©2005 Jonelle Weaver

Illustrations copyright ©2005 Lana Lê

Library of Congress Cataloging-in-Publication Data
Neumeier, Sara.
    Cupcakes year-round : 50 recipes for every season and celebration / Sara Neumeier ;
    photographs by Jonelle Weaver.
      p. cm.
    ISBN-13: 978-1-58479-403-5
    ISBN-10: 1-58479-403-8
      1. Cake. I. Title.
TX771.N48 2005
641.8'653–dc22   2004028722

Editor: **Beth Huseman**
Design & Illustration: **woolypear**
Food Stylist: **Sara Neumeier**
Prop Stylists: **Paige Hicks & Lana Lê**
Photographer's Assistant: **Nura Qureshi**
Production: **Alexis Mentor**

Special thanks to Rita Bobry and Anita Merk for their generous lending of props

The text of this book was composed in Claredon & House-a-rama League Night

Printed and bound in China

10 9 8 7 6 5 4 3

HNA
harry n. abrams, inc.
a subsidiary of La Martinière Groupe

115 West 18th Street
New York, NY 10011
www.hnabooks.com

cupcakes
YEAR-ROUND

50 Recipes for Every Season and Celebration

Sara Neumeier

PHOTOGRAPHS BY Jonelle Weaver

STEWART, TABORI & CHANG
NEW YORK

acknowledgments

This book all begins with an idea from editor Melanie Falick, whom I would like to thank for assembling the following team.

Lana Lê, whose charming page designs and whimsical illustrations set the tone for the book. Much of the structure spun from her visual concepts, and her constant creative feedback along the way kept the idea going.

Jonelle Weaver is responsible for the beautiful photographs. Her input and focus on the photo shoot was invaluable. Thanks to the organized and good-natured Paige Hicks for planning the shoot and providing many of the props.

And finally our wonderful editor Beth Huseman, who helped us keep the idea simple and cohesive and always managed to come up with just the right solution every time I hit a glitch.

contents

source guide

If you don't live near a good kitchen supply store, all of the cupcake equipment recommended in this book can be ordered online or by phone through any of the purveyors listed below. Wilton's website has the most extensive selection of baking papers and cupcake decorations.

Bakers Tools
www.bakerstools.com
(866) 285-2665

Bridge Kitchenware
www.bridgekitchenware.com
(212) 688-4220

Candyland Crafts
www.candylandcrafts.com
(908) 685-0410

Cooking.com
www.cooking.com
(800) 663-8810

New York Cake Supplies
www.nycake.com
(800) 942-2539

Pattycakes
www.pattycakes.com
(866) 999-8400

Sur La Table
www.surlatable.com
(800) 243-0852

Wilton
www.wilton.com
(800) 794-5866

Williams-Sonoma
www.williams-sonoma.com
(877) 812-6235

Chocolate connoisseurs will be able to find their favorite brands of chocolate at the first two websites listed below. The French company Valrhona and the American company Scharffen Berger produce some of the finest chocolates around. Large blocks of baking chocolates can be ordered directly from their websites.

Chocosphere
www.chocosphere.com
(877) 992-4626

Chocolate Source
www.chocolatesource.com
(800) 214-4926

Scharffen Berger
www.scharffenberger.com
(800) 930-4528

Valrhona
www.valrhona.com

mix & match

more ideas...

Jam Cupcakes
+
Brown Sugar Buttercream

Berry Crème Caramels

Jam Cupcakes
+
Chocolate Glaze

Chocolate Covered Strawberries

One Bowl Vanilla
+
Espresso/Brandy Syrup
+
Cream Cheese Icing
+
Chocolate Shavings

Tiramisu

Chocolate Cupcakes
+
Espresso Syrup
+
Whipped Chocolate Ganache
+
Crushed Espresso Beans

Mocha Bombshells

One Bowl Chocolate Cupcakes
+
Peanut Butter Icing
+
chopped toasted peanuts

Chocolate-Peanut Butter Cups

Chocolate Sour Cream Cupcakes
+
Brown Sugar Buttercream

Chocolate Downfalls

Chocolate Sour Cream Cupcakes
+
Rum Syrup
+
Caramel Icing

Chocolate-Caramel Delirium

Red Velvet Cupcakes
+
Easy Chocolate Buttercream
+
white and red candies

Poker Cupcakes

introduction

Remember when you were a little kid and you could hardly wait to eat the cupcakes that your mother made? Chances are, no matter what age you are now, you still feel the same way. A tray of cupcakes brings a surge of joy to four-year-olds and grandparents alike. Children love cupcakes because the size seems especially designed for them, and adults love cupcakes because they remind them of being children.

Perhaps some of the emotional satisfaction of eating cupcakes is the idea of getting an individual dessert, just for you. It could be that secretly, like little kids, we are delighted not to have to share. And then there's that delicious moment of peeling back the paper—it's just like opening a present.

As much fun as cupcakes are to eat, they are even more fun to make. They are quick and easy, leaving more time for the real adventure: decorating. Unlike icing a layer cake, decorating cupcakes is a great creative group project. Each one is a vehicle for expression. There is something intimate and special about receiving a cupcake that someone else has decorated for you. It makes you feel loved in the same way receiving a homemade, hand-drawn greeting card does.

Small, individually decorated cakes have been made and eaten for centuries. However, the tender, fluffy confection we now consider to be the classic cupcake didn't come into existence until the late 1800s, when chemical leaveners like baking soda, cream of tartar, and baking powder became widely available, making it possible to bake an airy cake. Before that baked goods were lightened with beaten eggs, resulting in cakes that were spongy rather than soft. Other cakes were dense, heavy affairs, lightened with yeast, or sometimes only by the air beaten into the butter.

Even with the new leaveners, baking cupcakes in the 1800s and early 1900s wasn't the casual task it is today. Batters had to be laboriously beaten by hand, and a baker might judge the oven temperature by holding their hand in the oven. It wasn't always easy to obtain ingredients like butter and sugar. In the early 1900s the commercial bakeries Drake's and Continental Baking Company

mix & match

Here are more yummy combinations to try. You can also experiment with pairings of your favorite flavors.

Apple Cupcakes
+
Streusel
+
Chantilly Cream

Apple Cobbler Cupcakes

Apple Cupcakes
+
Brandy Syrup
+
Stabilized Whipped Cream

Apple Blossoms

Blueberry Cupcakes
+
Maple Walnut Topping

New England Morning-Cupcakes

Coconut Cupcakes
+
Whipped Chocolate Ganache
+
toasted chopped almonds

Mounds Bars

Orange Buttermilk Cupcakes
+
Lemon Syrup
+
Honey Buttercream
+
chopped candied ginger

Citrus-Ginger Drops

Zucchini Cupcakes
+
Chocolate Glaze

August Afternoon Cupcakes

Hummingbird Cupcakes
+
Rum Syrup
+
Coconut Buttercream

Piña Colada Cupcakes

Hummingbird Cupcakes
+
Malted Milk Icing

Tropical Malted

became enormously successful selling pre-made cupcakes such as Ring Dings, Devil Dogs, and Hostess Twinkies.

People still love cupcakes enough to keep Drake's, Hostess, and a number of other companies in business. But with today's modern equipment and easy access to good ingredients, it's a trifle to whip out your own cupcakes. Once you grow accustomed to homemade cupcakes it's hard to go back to the chemical sweetness of packaged cupcakes or instant cake mix.

The cupcakes in this book range from a fast one-bowl cake recipe with creamed butter icing with (about 20 minutes hands-on time) to chocolate ganache covered cupcakes with gold-leafed chocolate shards on top (about 40 minutes hands-on time). Every cupcake can be kept simple, or embellished to your taste with flavored syrups, fillings, or fancy decorations.

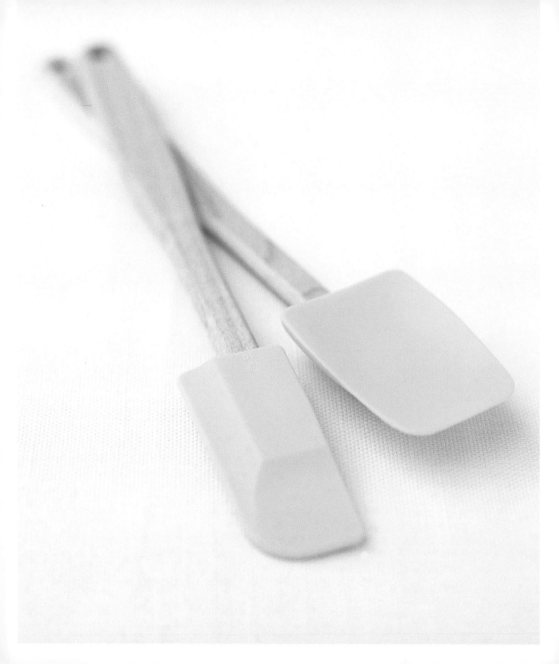

Cinnamon fans will love these coffee-cake-like cupcakes.

Those who don't like nuts can make an extra half recipe of streusel.

Sprinkle it over the tops of the cupcakes just before baking.

maple cinnamon cupcakes

1 recipe raw Buttermilk Cupcake batter (page 22)

1 recipe Cinnamon Streusel (page 53)

1 recipe Maple Walnut Topping (page 53)

Line 24 cupcake tins with baking papers. Fill each cupcake paper one-third full of batter. Sprinkle the streusel evenly over the batter. Fill the tins with the remaining batter. Bake until a skewer inserted in the middle of a cupcake comes out clean, 20 to 22 minutes. Set aside to cool, about 20 minutes.

Top each cupcake with a generous spoonful of Maple Walnut Topping.

MAKES 24 CUPCAKES

tools & supplies

One of the most defining characteristics of cupcakes is the frilly paper. They make cupcakes into finger food and preserve their moistness—otherwise, such tiny cupcakes would go stale quickly. But anyone who has embarked on a large cupcake project knows their greatest asset: no pan scrubbing. It's unnecessary to clean your cupcake pans between batches, just put in fresh papers. Most large, chain supermarkets carry pastel-colored baking papers. For white, brown, metallic, multicolored, or patterned papers see the Source Guide on page 104.

Then you will need cupcake tins and a good mixer. Tins range from the expensive heavy duty kind to disposable aluminum ones. There isn't a huge difference in the outcome, only which pan will last longer. Most everyone owns a hand-held electric mixer, which will work for all the recipes in this book. However, your life will be made much easier with a freestanding mixer. A standing mixer holds the bowl and the beaters for you, leaving you free to measure sugar, whisk egg whites, melt chocolate, or answer the phone.

Have a few basic tools on hand before you start baking: measuring spoons, dry measuring cups, a liquid measuring cup, a rubber spatula, cupcake papers, and a cooling rack. This will save you from rummaging around cupboards with flour-covered fingers in the midst of sifting, creaming, or folding.

A few extras can make the fast and easy process of baking cupcakes even faster and easier. An ice cream scoop is wonderfully handy for filling cupcake tins. It measures the right amount of batter for one cupcake, and then neatly deposits it into a baking paper without getting any on the side of the pan. A three-ounce scoop will measure the right amount of batter for a medium cupcake. If you only have a four-ounce scoop, fill the scoop a little less.

As for frosting, a butter knife is the classic tool and does a fine job. But for fast, neat frosting nothing is more efficient than a small offset spatula. These little wonders have a flat rounded blade designed especially for even spreading. A crooked handle adds leverage, and keeps your fingers out of the frosting. Although maybe you don't want to! Small offset spatulas measure about 5 inches long, and can be found in most kitchen supply stores.

What better excuse to make these old-fashioned scarlet-crumbed cakes than Valentines day! Although traditional red velvet cake has bright white icing, you can tint your icing pink for a little extra holiday spirit. Adorn your cakes with cupcake-sized Valentines' cards and you have the perfect gift. Buy miniature heart-shaped cards, or cut your own out of red paper.

red velvet valentines

1   recipe Red Velvet Cupcakes (see page 35)

1   recipe Cream Cheese Icing (see page 44)

    Red or pink food coloring (optional)

24   two-to-three-inch Valentines' Day cards

Tint the icing pink with a small amount red or pink food coloring, if desired. Using an offset spatula, frost the cupcakes with the Cream Cheese icing. Garnish each with a card.

MAKES 24 CUPCAKES

More ambitious cupcake decorators may want to invest in some pastry bags, couplers, and pastry tips. A ten to twelve inch pastry bag is the most useful size. It will hold a generous amount of icing without being too bulky too handle. A coupler consists of a conical plastic tube that fits into your pastry bag. A matching nut allows you to screw different pastry tips onto the outside of the bag, so you don't have to empty out the bag every time you want to insert a new tip. Pastry bags can be bought in most kitchen supply stores. Couplers and tips are sold online and in cake decorating stores. They come individually and in kits.

red velvet valentine

Linzertorte is a German dessert often served during the winter holidays. Usually it is quite fancy, with bright red jam peeking out from under a latticework crust. These bite sized versions are much quicker to make, but are still very elegant.

linzer cupcakes

2 cups seedless raspberry jam

1 recipe mini Browned Butter Nut Cupcakes (page 26)

48 small almond or shortbread cookies (1 per cupcake)

1/2 cup confectioners' sugar, for sifting

Place the jam in a small bowl set over a small pan of gently simmering water. Stir the jam over the heat until it is liquid, about 4 minutes. Spread a thin layer of jam over the top of each cupcake.

Arrange the cookies in a single layer on a baking tray. Sift confectioners' sugar over the cookies. Place one cookie, sugar side up, on top of each cupcake.

MAKES 48 MINI CUPCAKES

understanding & using ingredients

For the sake of uniformity, all the recipes in this book call for large eggs. When making cake batter or meringue, it is always best to have the eggs at room temperature. They will hold more air, and combine more easily with the other ingredients. However, for recipes that require eggs to be separated, you will find it is easier to separate eggs when they are cold, as the proteins which hold the eggs together are firmer, making the membrane around the yolk less likely to break. Separate the eggs while cold, and then bring them to room temperature.

When whipping egg whites to fold into cake batter, start with a clean bowl and whisk. Any grease or bits of yolk will keep your egg whites from volumizing. If, while separating, you do get a little bit of yolk in with your egg whites, it is not necessary to toss out all the whites and start over. Simply scoop the yolk out, along with the white surrounding it, and replace the removed amount with the white from another egg.

FATS

Fats are what keep a cupcake moist and help distribute flavor to your taste buds. All the cupcakes in this book are either butter or oil based. Commercial bakeries often use hydrogenated shortenings like Crisco. These shortenings hold more air when creamed, producing an extremely light cake. If lightness is your main concern, feel free to substitute shortening for butter in the creamed butter recipes in this book. However, you may miss the wonderful flavor of butter.

When oil is called for in a recipe, use one with a neutral flavor, such as safflower, corn, or sunflower. Oil is one of those ingredients that tends to stay in your cupboard for a long time, and it can go rancid eventually. So smell your oil before baking with it. Any unpleasant or acrid odor will permeate the flavor of your cupcakes. It may be worth starting with a fresh bottle of oil.

linzer cupcakes

Leavening is what causes your cupcakes to rise. Most of the cupcakes in this book are leavened with baking soda, double-acting baking powder, or a combination of the two. Baking soda reacts with acidic ingredients like buttermilk, sour cream, molasses, or brown sugar. Double-acting baking powder is baking soda that has the acids built in. The first part of the "double-action," takes place when the baking powder reacts with moisture in the batter, lightening the raw batter with tiny gas bubbles. The greater reaction occurs in the oven. Because double-action baking powder is mostly heat activated, it's fine to stand batters leavened solely with baking powder in the fridge an hour or so before baking. However, baking soda starts reacting as soon as it gets wet and doesn't stop. Cupcakes leavened solely with baking soda must be baked immediately or the power of the baking soda will dissipate before ever reaching the oven.

EXTRACTS

Most baked goods contain the secret ingredient of pure vanilla or pure almond extract. But remember to keep it a secret! Too much extract can be overpowering. Almond is particularly strong. Extract should only serve to support the other flavors in your batter, not steal the show.

Always use pure vanilla extract and not imitation. Imitation is cheaper but worthless. Instead of adding a wonderful flowery, nutty aroma, it adds a horrible chemical taste only vaguely reminiscent of the real thing. Imitation vanilla is responsible for the disturbing chemical flavor in instant cake mixes, and is the major reason making cupcakes by scratch is really worth it. So if that flavor doesn't bother you, you may as well use a mix. In any instance, there is no reason to ever purchase a bottle of imitation vanilla extract.

CITRUS ZEST

The thin, colored skin that surrounds the pith of a citrus fruit contains a more concentrated flavor than the actual juice, without the acids that will alter the chemistry of your cake batter. While the juice of a citrus fruit is flavorful, much of the flavor is simply the tartness of the juice. If you want a stronger citrus

The holiday beverage hot buttered rum is a decadent combination of steaming rum, butter and sugar, said to "make a man see double and feel single." For all of the flavor and nearly none of the alcohol, try this dessert.

hot buttered rum cupcakes

1 recipe Buttermilk Cupcakes (page 22)

1 recipe Rum Syrup (page 51)

1 recipe Brown Sugar Buttercream (page 39)

Brush the tops of cupcakes generously with syrup. Frost with the buttercream.

MAKES 24 CUPCAKES

flavor in your cake or icing you'll get most of what you want from the zest. Citrus curds require the acid of citrus juice to thicken, but adding a little zest will make them even more flavorful.

It used to be that grating zest was a painstaking process, with most of the zest remaining caught in the holes of the fine side of your box grater. Not anymore! Most kitchen supply stores now sell long, rasp-like graters (such as the Microplane), which make grating zest a joy.

CHOCOLATE

Most of the recipes in this book that call for chocolate will work well with the regular semi-sweet chocolate chips or unsweetened chocolate found in supermarkets. Although these may bring a sneer to the lips of French pastry chefs, chocolate chips have a flavor that is very close to the heart of most Americans. If you are a chocolate connoisseur who is willing to seek out high-grade chocolate, go ahead and make the substitution. For suppliers of Valrhona, Callebaut, and other high-grade chocolates, see the Source Guide (page 104).

The one recipe that calls for high-grade chocolate is the recipe for Fallen Leaves, because it requires the chocolate to be tempered. Tempering is the process of melting chocolate very slowly, so that it will harden back up nicely when cooled. If chocolate is gets too hot (above 120°F for dark chocolate, 110°F for white chocolate) the fat will separate from the rest of the chocolate. Once this happens, the chocolate will no longer cool to its original hardness. Instead of sitting beautifully on your cupcakes, your Fallen Leaves will droop or worse, melt. Store-bought chocolate chips have emulsifiers added which make them difficult to temper.

MILK, BUTTERMILK, AND SOUR CREAM

Most cake batters call for some kind of liquid to bind the dry ingredients together and help activate the leaveners. Milk is always preferable to water as the fats and enzymes in it keep the cupcakes moist and soft. Many of the recipes in this book call for buttermilk or sour cream. These have acids in them that keep the flour from getting tough, and make exceptionally tender cupcakes.

Every Christmas in Britain bakeries are full of dense fruit cakes covered in a stiff sugar icing. Although the word "fruitcake" evokes Christmas in America, the heaviness of traditional fruitcake is not popular here. These cakes have the rich, spicy flavor of British fruitcakes, but a light, fluffy texture.

mini fruit cupcakes

1	recipe Quick Fruit Cupcakes (page 34)
1	recipe Brandy Syrup (page 51; optional)
1	recipe Almond Sugar Glaze (page 42)
	Green Fruit Rollups
48 to 72	red candies such as red M&Ms (2 or 3 per cupcake)

Brush the tops of the cupcakes generously with syrup, if desired. Using an offset spatula, evenly spread the top of each cupcake with 1 1/2 tablespoons icing, reserving a small amount of icing to attach decorations. Let the cupcakes sit until the icing hardens slightly.

Meanwhile, use kitchen shears to cut the Fruit Rollups into 24 leaf shapes. Dab the end of one leaf in the reserved icing, and place the leaf in the top of a cupcake. Use a little icing to attach two or three red candies around the base of the leaf to look like holly berries. Repeat with the remaining cupcakes.

MAKES 24 CUPCAKES

cupcake science:
mixing, filling, baking & icing

MIXING

Superlative cupcakes begin with the mixing process. The most common method of mixing is the creaming method. This allows air to get into the cupcakes twice. The creaming method begins by beating butter and sugar together until fluffy. The mixture will expand in size and become pale from all the air bubbles trapped in it. Add the room temperature eggs one at a time. You add them one at a time so that the egg will emulsify with the butter mixture. When you add cold eggs, or too much egg at a time, the mixture will curdle and lose some of its lightness. You do all this beating before adding the flour, because if you over-beat the flour the gluten proteins in the flour will join together to form long strands, making the cupcakes dense and tough once baked. Once the batter goes into the oven, the chemical leaveners in the batter react dramatically with the heat and emit gasses that make the cupcakes rise. Because the batter is already full of air, the cupcakes rise easily to have a nice even crumb.

A few recipes in this book are made using the one bowl method, where the dry ingredients are combined, and the wet ingredients are whisked right in. Cupcakes made from this method tend be slightly heavier but bake with a nice high dome.

FILLING

Ever bake cupcakes from a recipe in an old cookbook and find that it didn't make as many cupcakes as promised? That's because the old-fashioned style of cupcake was smaller. The cupcake papers were filled less to emphasize the dainty ruffled edges of the papers. Today's cupcakes tend to be more about abundance than delicacy. Filling your cupcake papers $2/3$ to $3/4$ full will result in a happy balance between the two styles: a generously sized cupcake with just a bit of a paper ruffle around the edge.

These are a delicious play on Hostess snowballs. You can choose to dye your coconut "snow" in playful colors, or just leave it white. Serve the finished snowballs in a mound, or present each one in a clean baking paper.

snowballs

1 recipe Buttermilk, Chocolate, or Coconut Cupcakes (pages 22, 24, 27)

1 recipe Rum Syrup (page 51; optional)

1 recipe Swiss Meringue Buttercream or Brown Sugar Buttercream (pages 38 or 39)

8 cups sweetened coconut flakes

Food coloring of your choice (optional)

Brush the tops of the cupcakes generously with syrup, if using. Unwrap the cupcakes and arrange them on two baking sheets that will fit in your freezer. Place the cupcakes in the freezer to chill, about 30 minutes.

Meanwhile, make the colored coconut "snow." If you plan to make three different colors, get out three medium mixing bowls; if making one color, you'll need one large bowl. Place 1/4 cup water in each of the three bowls, or 1/2 cup in the large bowl. Add a small amount of desired food coloring to each of the bowls. To test the intensity of your color, dip a few shreds of coconut into the colored water. If the color is too pale, add more food coloring. If the color is too intense, start again. When you have your colors as you would like them, add the coconut—one third to each of the medium bowls, or all the coconut to the large bowl.

Remove the cupcakes from the freezer. Using an offset spatula, frost the cupcakes on top and all the way around. Once a cupcake is frosted, place it back in the freezer to firm up. When all the cupcakes are frosted and the frosting is firm, roll them in the coconut.

MAKES 24 CUPCAKES

Most ovens heat from the bottom. For this reason, it is important to let your oven preheat for at least 20 minutes. The intense heat that your oven gives off while preheating is likely to burn the bottoms of your cupcakes. However, some of us have ovens that burn the bottoms of things anyway. If this is the case with your oven place a sturdy pan directly under your cupcake tin. This will help insulate your tin and distribute the heat more evenly. Most ovens tend to brown a little faster in the back than the front. Check your cupcakes after 12 minutes. If they are browning unevenly rotate the pans.

Because cupcakes have such a short baking time, three minutes more or less can make all the difference. If the cupcakes are underdone, they will sink a little in the middle and be too moist in the center. If they are overdone they will be dry on the outside. Most cupcakes take between 18 and 22 minutes to bake, so start checking them after 17 minutes. A done cupcake will be firm to the touch, and a wooden skewer inserted into the center will be free of any sticky cake crumbs when removed.

ICING

It's hard to be patient when you're waiting for a delicious batch of cupcakes to cool for icing. But you must wait until they are completely cool. Any heat emanating from the cupcakes will warm up the butter in your icing, make a runny mess, and you will waste time instead of saving it.

TAKING YOUR CUPCAKES ONE STEP FURTHER: SYRUPS, FILLINGS & DECORATIONS

If your cupcakes are going be hanging around for more than a couple days, it might be worth brushing them with a little flavored sugar syrup before frosting them. Sugar syrups are made by boiling sugar and water together until the sugar is dissolved and the syrup is slightly thickened. They can be flavored with rum, liquor, citrus juice, or espresso. Use a pastry brush to apply syrup generously to the tops of cooled cupcakes. Not only do syrups add another flavor dimension to your cupcakes, they help them stay moist longer, acting as a sort of natural preservative.

snowballs

Have you ever bitten into a filled cupcake and wondered, "How does the filling get in there?" Here's one easy way. Fill a pastry bag with your choice of fillings. Poke a hole in the center of a baked cupcake with a knife. Insert the pastry bag into the hole, and fill. At least one-and-a-half tablespoons of filling should be able to fit into the cupcake. Delicious cupcake fillings include sweetened mascarpone cheese, citrus curds, whipped ganache, or stabilized whipped cream, or you can use ready-made spreads such as jam or Nutella.

The classic decoration for cupcakes is a colorful sprinkling of jimmies or non-pareils. But if you want some variation try chocolate shavings, toasted coconut, crushed nuts or cookies, or chopped up candies like toffee or torrone.

In my family we left Santa's reindeer a snack of cheese and crackers the night before Christmas. I always wondered if the reindeer wouldn't prefer a dessert.

The crushed peppermint "snow" adorning these cakes makes decorating easy. These festive cakes are a good way to make use of surplus candy canes. It's wise to crush your candy canes right before you want to use them — any humidity can cause the crushed candy to clump.

reindeer snacks

1 recipe Chocolate Sour Cream Cupcakes (page 25)

1 recipe Swiss Meringue Buttercream (page 38)

1 cup finely crushed peppermint candy (about 12 medium candy canes)

Stir $\frac{1}{2}$ cup of the peppermint candy into the buttercream. Using an offset spatula, frost the cupcakes. Sprinkle the remaining crushed peppermints over the tops of the cupcakes.

MAKES 24 CUPCAKES

piping techniques

For those who love the visual aspect of baking, this book includes a few recipes which require basic piping skills. Before you embark on your piping adventure, here's what you should have on hand: one 10-to-12-inch pastry bag for every color of frosting you want to use, one coupler for every bag and either a full set of pastry tips or the few that you know you'd like to use, paper towels for cleaning fingers, and an offset spatula for smoothing icing surfaces and scraping off mistakes.

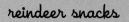

If coloring your icing, there are several options. The liquid vegetable dye sold in supermarkets will work well, but you may have to do a bit more mixing to get the exact shade that you want. Paste food coloring is made especially for pastry chefs and comes in beautiful colors (see the Source Guide on page 104). If coloring Swiss meringue buttercream, be aware that it doesn't absorb yellow as easily as the other colors. You may have to use twice as much as you expect.

Test the strength of your food coloring by adding a very small amount to your icing. If you are using paste food coloring, start with just tiny bit on the end of a toothpick. Keep stirring in color gradually, taking into consideration that as your icing sits the color will intensify slightly.

To fill your pastry bag, hold the bag open with one hand, folding the top edges of the bag over your hand. Using a rubber spatula carefully dollop frosting into the bottom of the bag near the tip. Try to keep the top part of the bag clean. Gently shake the bag to make sure the filling shifts down to the bottom of the bag and there are no air pockets.

Never fill your bag more than two thirds full, or you may find icing oozing out of the top of the bag in the middle of piping. Twist the top part of the bag to close making sure not to introduce any air. Use your right hand to hold the bag right below the twist. This hand will apply the pressure, which controls the flow of the icing. Use your left hand to guide your pastry tip and steady the bag.

If you are bold enough to pipe directly on your cupcakes, more power to you. But for many people, even professional pastry chefs, there is a moment of stage fright before piping on a cake. The solution is to practice piping on a cutting board or other kitchen surface first. Don't worry about wasting icing, you can simply scrape up the piped icing you and put it back in the pastry bag. Keep practicing until you feel comfortable.

winter

PIPING LEAVES

Use pastry tips #66 and #67 for piping small leaves, and tips #68 and #69 to pipe wider leaves such as the squash leaves on page 69. Start at the base of the leaf, and ease upon the pressure as you lift the pastry bag up. This creates a leaf with a wide base and a thin, pointed top.

PIPING A SIMPLE FLOWER

Use pastry tip #104 to create a simple medium sized flower, such as the hibiscus on page 55. Use a toothpick or skewer to mark where you would like the center of the flower to be. Position the pastry tip with the wide side touching the center mark. Apply even pressure and draw pastry tip $3/4$ inch out from the center of the cupcake to form one side of a petal. When you've made one side of the petal as long as desired, continue applying pressure keeping the wide end of the pastry tip stationary on the cupcake and swiveling the narrow end of the pastry tip to form the round end of the flower petal. Draw the wide end of the pastry tip back toward the center of the cupcake, making sure the piping joins up with the first half of the petal. Repeat to create the remaining petals, making sure that the petals are evenly spaced out. Apply yellow jimmies or a small round candy to create a stamen-like center.

PIPING LETTERS

Cupcakes with letters piped on them are a popular way to spell out birthday, anniversary, or holiday greetings. Plain pastry tips #3 and #4 create finer lines, and are recommended for pipers with confident, steady hands. For larger, block lettering use tips #5 or #6.

To create the lowercase font used on page 86, use the back of a pastry tip to gently mark where you want the rounded edges of the letters to be. Use a skewer or toothpick to mark where the flat edges should be. Use these marks as a guide to pipe the letters.

This cupcake was originally "Chocolate Whoppers", but Malted Milk Icing overpowered the chocolate. I decided to let the icing steal the show. The Brandy Syrup supports the nuttiness of the malted milk flavor very nicely.

vanilla whoppers

1   recipe One-Bowl Vanilla Cupcakes
    (page 23)

1   recipe Brandy Syrup
    (page 51; optional)

1   recipe Malted Milk Icing
    (page 44)

$1/2$ cup chopped torrone, or

$1/3$ cup chopped peanuts

Generously brush the tops of the cupcakes with syrup, if using. Frost the cupcakes with Malted Milk Icing, and sprinkle the tops of cupcakes with the torrone.

MAKES 24 CUPCAKES

The fresh apples in these rich, moist cakes make these a more wholesome variety of dessert, as long as you don't count the incredibly decadent caramel icing on top!

apple cupcakes

1   recipe Apple Cupcakes
    (page 33)

1   recipe Caramel Filling
    and Icing (page 46)

Glaze the cupcakes with Caramel Icing. Let the icing get firm before serving, about 30 minutes.

MAKES 24 CUPCAKES

packaging cupcakes for travel

The key to safely transporting cupcakes is to chill or even freeze them beforehand. This firms the cupcakes enough so that they can endure mild jostling without getting smashed. The easiest packaging for cupcakes is right in their own baking tins. The individual cups separate the cupcakes and protect them from sliding into one another, and you can easily cover the whole thing with foil for transport. This works well provided you have as many tins as cupcakes and enough hands to carry each tin separately.

For large cupcake projects, you may have to procure 4-to-5-inch-tall plastic-ware or cardboard cake boxes. Cake boxes can be found at baking and kitchen supply stores, or you may be able to buy some from your local bakery. For casually decorated cupcakes, place your chilled cupcakes snugly in the bottom of a box. Pad any unfilled space between the cupcakes and edges of the box with crumpled up paper towels, or folded strips of bubble wrap. As long as the boxes are handled with care, the cupcakes will arrive at their destination intact. If you are transporting extremely elaborate or delicate cupcakes, don't take any chances—freeze them. Place half-a-piece of crumpled up paper towel in between each cupcake to keep them from sliding around.

You do want your cupcakes to come to room temperature before they are eaten. This takes about 40 minutes for refrigerated cupcakes, and 2 hours for frozen cupcakes. The time the journey takes will most likely be long enough to thaw them. If you have a hard time keeping ravenous cupcake-eaters at bay, remind them that the best things in life are worth waiting for.

What could be more appropriate for a spelling bee than honey-flavored alphabet cupcakes? To make all the letters of the alphabet, you will have to bake two extra cupcakes. When baking your cupcakes, fill all the cupcake papers just a bit scant to make the batter come out to 26. The baking time will be a couple minutes shorter.

spelling bee alphabet cupcakes

1   recipe Buttermilk Cupcakes (page 22)

1   recipe Honey Lemon Syrup (page 52; optional)

1¹/₂   recipes Honey Buttercream (page 39)

Red food coloring; or another bright color

Transfer 1¹/₂ cups of the buttercream to a medium bowl. Add enough food coloring to make a vibrant color to pipe with.

Generously brush the tops of the cupcakes with syrup, if using. Using an offset spatula, frost the cupcakes with buttercream, making sure that the top is flat and smooth enough to pipe on.

Fit a pastry bag with a plain round #3 to #6 pastry tip. Pipe the letters A through Z on top of the cupcakes (see page 19).

MAKES 26 CUPCAKES

basic cupcake recipes

spelling bee alphabet cupcakes

buttermilk cupcakes

- 3 cups cake flour
- 1 teaspoon baking powder
- $1/2$ teaspoon baking soda
- $1/2$ teaspoon salt
- $1^1/2$ cups (3 sticks) unsalted butter, at room temperature
- 2 cups sugar
- 4 large eggs
- 2 teaspoons pure vanilla extract
- $1^1/3$ cups buttermilk

Preheat the oven to 350°F. Line 24 cupcake tins with baking papers. Sift together the flour, baking powder, baking soda, and salt. Set aside.

In the bowl of an electric mixer, cream together the butter and sugar until fluffy, about 3 minutes. Add the eggs, one at a time, beating well after each addition. Stir in the vanilla. Alternately add the flour mixture and buttermilk, beginning and ending with the flour.

Fill each baking cup two-thirds full. Bake until a skewer inserted into the middle of a cupcake comes out clean, about 20 minutes.

MAKES 24 CUPCAKES

citrus flavor variation

TO MAKE LEMON, ORANGE, OR LIME BUTTERMILK CUPCAKES

Follow instructions for Buttermilk Cupcakes and beat in the grated zest of one lemon, one orange, or two limes with the butter and sugar.

With their Fudgie Brownie bodies, chocolate ganache frosting, and licorice legs, these spiders are definitely more scared of you than you are of them.

scuttling spiders

1 recipe mini Fudgie Brownie Cupcakes (page 36)

1/2 recipe Whipped Chocolate Ganache (page 47; prepare no more than 1 hour before frosting)

1 package shoestring licorice (the curly kind makes the best spider legs)

96 candy dots, Red Hots, or other small round candies (2 per cupcake)

Cut the licorice into 1 1/2 inch lengths (you'll need 192 pieces to make legs for 24 spiders). Fit a pastry bag with a plain round #10 pastry tip. Pipe a dome of ganache on a cupcake that's large enough to cover most of the top of the cupcake. While the ganache is still soft, stick pieces of licorice into the ganache, four on each side, so that the licorice resembles spider legs. Place two round candies on the front of the spider to resemble eyes. Do not attempt to move the spider until the ganache is firm, or the legs may fall off. Repeat with the remaining cupcakes.

MAKES 48 MINI CUPCAKES

one-bowl vanilla cupcakes

1½ cups (3 sticks) unsalted butter

1½ cups packed light brown sugar

3 large eggs

1¼ cups milk

2 teaspoons pure vanilla extract

2 teaspoons baking powder

½ teaspoon salt

3 cups cake flour

Preheat the oven to 350°F. Line 24 cupcake tins with baking papers. Place the butter in a medium, heatproof bowl placed over a pot of gently simmering water. When the butter is just melted, whisk in the brown sugar. Let cool to lukewarm temperature, about 4 minutes.

Whisk the eggs into the mixture. Add the milk, vanilla, baking powder, and salt; whisk to combine. Whisk in the flour until evenly combined.

Fill each baking paper two-thirds full. Bake until a skewer inserted into the middle of a cupcake comes out clean, about 20 minutes.

MAKES 24 CUPCAKES

The web design on these cupcakes looks complicated, but don't worry. It's just an ingenious French pastry technique. The spider webs must be piped while the glaze is still wet, so you must decorate one cupcake at a time.

spider webs

1 recipe Chocolate Sour Cream Cupcakes (page 25)

1 recipe Brandy Syrup or Espresso Syrup (page 51; optional)

1 recipe Chocolate Glaze (page 47), kept warm

$1/4$ recipe White Chocolate for Piping (page 46), kept warm

Brush the tops of the cupcakes generously with syrup, if using. Fit a pastry bag with a #3 plain pastry tip. Fill the bag with the white chocolate. Using an offset spatula, spread an even layer of glaze over the top of one cupcake. While the glaze is still runny, pipe a spiral of white chocolate, starting from the middle of the cupcake and working outward.

Using a skewer or toothpick, gently drag a line from the center of the spiral to the outer edge of the cupcake. Pipe five or six more lines radiating out from the center of the spiral, making sure to space them evenly like the spokes in a wheel. Repeat the process with the remaining cupcakes. If your white chocolate becomes too cool to pipe, lay your pastry bag in a bowl set over a pot of gently simmering water until it becomes fluid again. Let the glaze on your cupcakes become firm before serving, about 40 minutes.

MAKES 24 CUPCAKES

one-bowl chocolate cupcakes

Four 1-ounce squares unsweetened baking chocolate

$1/2$ cup (1 stick) unsalted butter

1 cup hot water

2 cups sugar

2 large eggs

$1/2$ cup buttermilk

1 teaspoon pure vanilla extract

$1/4$ teaspoon salt

$1^{1}/_4$ teaspoon baking soda

2 cups all-purpose flour

Preheat the oven to 350°F. Line 24 cupcakes tins with baking papers. Place the chocolate, butter, and boiling water in a medium, heatproof bowl placed over a pot of gently simmering water. When the chocolate and butter are just melted, whisk in the sugar. Let cool to lukewarm temperature, about 4 minutes.

Whisk the eggs into the mixture. Add the buttermilk, vanilla, salt, and baking soda; whisk to combine. Whisk in the flour until evenly combined.

Fill each baking paper two-thirds full. Bake until a skewer inserted into the middle of a cupcake comes out clean, about 20 minutes.

MAKES 24 CUPCAKES

chocolate sour cream cupcakes

2 cups all-purpose flour

1³/₄ cups sugar

1¹/₂ teaspoons baking soda

¹/₄ teaspoon salt

Four 1-ounce squares unsweetened baking chocolate

1 cup (2 sticks) unsalted butter

1 cup sour cream

4 large eggs

¹/₂ cup strong coffee

1 teaspoon pure vanilla extract

Preheat the oven to 350°F. Line 24 cupcake tins with baking papers. Sift together the flour, sugar, baking soda, and salt. Set aside.

In a large bowl placed over a saucepan of gently simmering water, melt together the chocolate and butter. Remove from heat. Whisk in the sour cream, eggs, coffee, and vanilla until well-combined. Add the flour mixture and whisk until evenly combined.

Fill each baking cup two-thirds full. Bake until a skewer inserted into the middle of a cupcake comes out clean, about 20 minutes.

MAKES 24 CUPCAKES

Moist jam cakes are filled with an extra squirt of jam in the center for a bright burst of flavor. Raspberry makes the best contrast with peanut butter icing.

pb & js

1 recipe Jam Cupcakes (page 28)

1 recipe Peanut Butter Buttercream (page 39)

1 cup seedless raspberry jam

$^1/_2$ cup raw unsalted peanuts

Preheat the oven to 350°F. Spread the peanuts evenly on a baking sheet. Bake until the peanuts are fragrant and slightly toasted, about 8 minutes. Transfer to a plate and let cool.

Insert a paring knife into the center of each cupcake to make a crevice. Fit a pastry bag with a plain round #8, #9, or #10 tip and fill the bag with jam. Pipe the jam into the crevices. Frost the cupcakes with the buttercream. Chop the reserved peanuts coarsely, and sprinkle them over the cupcakes.

MAKES 24 CUPCAKES

This cake batter is so rich, it's best baked as mini cupcakes.

browned butter nut cupcakes

1³/₄ cup unsalted butter

1 cup raw nuts, such as pistachios, almonds, or hazelnuts

3¹/₃ cups confectioners' sugar

1 cup plus 2 tablespoons all-purpose flour

12 egg whites

2 tablespoons honey

Preheat the oven to 375°F. Line 48 mini-cupcake tins with mini-baking papers. In a large saucepan, melt the butter over medium-high heat. When the butter begins to brown and gives off a nutty aroma, 7 to 10 minutes, transfer the brown butter to a heatproof bowl to stop the cooking.

Place the nuts and confectioners' sugar in a food processor. Pulse until the nuts are finely ground, about 4 minutes. Add the flour and pulse to combine.

In the bowl of an electric mixer, beat the egg whites until frothy. Add the nut mixture and whisk until combined. Whisk in the brown butter and the honey. Refrigerate at least 1 hour.

Fill each baking cup three-fourths full. Bake until the tops are golden and firm to the touch, about 18 minutes.

MAKES 48 MINI CUPCAKES

pb & js

coconut cupcakes

3 cups cake flour

1 teaspoon baking powder

1/2 teaspoon baking soda

1/2 teaspoon salt

4 large eggs

$1^{1}/_{2}$ cups (3 sticks) unsalted butter, at room temperature

2 cups sugar

$1^{1}/_{4}$ cups canned coconut cream

$^{1}/_{2}$ teaspoon almond extract

8 ounces sweetened coconut flakes

Preheat the oven to 350°F. Line 24 cupcake tins with baking papers. Sift together the flour, baking powder, baking soda, and salt. Set aside.

In the bowl of an electric mixer, cream together the butter and sugar until fluffy, about 3 minutes. Add the eggs, one at a time, beating well after each addition. Alternately add the flour and coconut cream to the mixture, beginning and ending with the flour. Stir in the almond extract and shredded coconut.

Fill each baking cup two-thirds full. Bake until a skewer inserted into the middle of a cupcake comes out clean, about 20 minutes.

MAKES 24 CUPCAKES

This is the gilded lily of chocolate cupcakes — for those too-much-is-not-enough types. Moist, sour cream chocolate cupcakes are flavored with Brandy Syrup, frosted with whipped ganache, and decorated with shards of chocolate. For upscale occasions apply gold leaf to your chocolate decorations (see page 45), and for a simpler version try dusting them with cocoa.

1   recipe Chocolate Sour Cream Cupcakes (page 25)

1   recipe Brandy Syrup or Espresso Syrup (page 51)

1   recipe Whipped Chocolate Ganache (page 47;
     prepare no more than 1 hour before frosting)

1   recipe Fallen Leaves (page 45; dusted with cocoa or gold-leaf)

Brush the tops of the cupcakes generously with syrup. Frost the cupcakes with ganache. While the ganache is still soft (it will stiffen later), place two or three Fallen Leaves on top of each cupcake.

MAKES 24 CUPCAKES

This recipe is an updated spin of a classic Southern cake. While the original recipe is a complex concoction using brown sugar and spices, this version has been kept simple to bring out the berry flavor in the jam. The jam keeps the cake moist and almost acts as a preservative.

jam cupcakes

2$\frac{1}{2}$ cups all-purpose flour

1 teaspoon baking soda

1/4 teaspoon salt

1 cup (2 sticks) unsalted butter, at room temperature

1$\frac{1}{2}$ cup sugar

4 large eggs, separated

1 cup buttermilk, at room temperature

1$\frac{3}{4}$ cups jam, such as seedless raspberry, strawberry, or blackberry

Preheat the oven to 350°F. Line 24 cupcake tins with baking papers. Sift together the flour, baking soda, and salt. Set aside.

In the bowl of an electric mixer, cream together the butter and sugar until fluffy, about 3 minutes. Add the egg yolks, one at a time, beating well after each addition. Alternately add the flour mixture and the buttermilk, beginning and ending with flour. Stir in the jam until just combined. Beat the reserved egg whites until stiff. Using a rubber spatula, gently fold them into the cake batter.

Fill each baking paper two-thirds full. Bake until a skewer inserted into the middle of a cupcake comes out clean, about 20 minutes.

MAKES 24 CUPCAKES

fallen leaves

blueberry cupcakes

1 cup (2 sticks) unsalted butter

1 cup packed light brown sugar

2 large eggs

$^1/_2$ cup milk

2 teaspoons pure vanilla extract

$^1/_2$ teaspoon salt

2 teaspoons baking powder

$1^1/_2$ cups cake flour

2 cups fresh blueberries

Preheat the oven to 350°F. Line 24 cupcake tins with baking papers. Place the butter in a medium heatproof bowl placed over a pot of gently simmering water. When the butter is just melted, whisk in the brown sugar. Let cool to lukewarm temperature, about 4 minutes.

Whisk the eggs into the butter-sugar mixture. Add the milk, vanilla, salt, and baking powder; whisk to combine. Whisk in the flour until just combined. Fold in the blueberries.

Fill each baking paper two-thirds full. Bake until a skewer inserted into the middle of a cupcake comes out clean, about 20 minutes.

MAKES 24 CUPCAKES

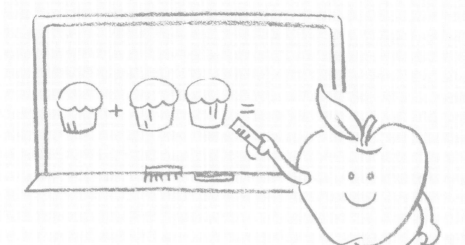

fall

carrot cupcakes

1 1/2   cups all-purpose flour

1 1/2   teaspoons baking soda

1 1/2   teaspoons ground cinnamon

1/2   teaspoon freshly grated nutmeg

1/2   teaspoon salt

3   large eggs

1 1/2   cups sugar

1 1/4   cup vegetable oil

2   teaspoons pure vanilla extract

2 1/2   cups grated carrots (6 to 8 medium carrots)

Preheat the oven to 350°F. Line 24 cupcake tins with baking papers. Sift together the flour, baking soda, cinnamon, nutmeg, and salt. Set aside.

Beat together the eggs and sugar. Add the oil and vanilla and beat to combine. Stir in the carrots. Add the flour mixture and stir to combine.

Fill each baking paper two-thirds full. Bake until a skewer inserted into the middle of a cupcake comes out clean, about 20 minutes.

MAKES 24 CUPCAKES

These cupcakes are mini-versions of the classic Southern American layer cake. Why is it called hummingbird cake? The most plausible story is that its sweetness attracts children like nectar attracts hummingbirds. Usually, Hummingbird Cake has little or no decoration, but to make your cupcakes a little more playful decorate them with a rosette of Cream Cheese Icing and a toasted pecan.

hummingbird cupcakes

24 pecans (1 per cupcake)

1 recipe Hummingbird Cupcakes (page 32)

1 recipe Cream Cheese Icing (page 44)

Preheat the oven to 350°F. Spread the pecans evenly on a baking sheet. Bake until fragrant and slightly toasted, about 8 minutes. Transfer to a plate and let cool. Fit a pastry bag with a large #16 star tip. Fill with the icing. Hold the tip above a cupcake at a 45-degree angle. Applying steady pressure, move the tip in a full circle. Ease up on the pressure while pulling up to finish the rosette. Repeat with the remaining cupcakes. Place a pecan in the center of each rosette.

MAKES 24 CUPCAKES

zucchini cupcakes

1 1/2 cups all-purpose flour

1 1/2 teaspoons baking soda

1 1/2 teaspoons ground ginger

1/2 teaspoon ground nutmeg

1/2 teaspoon salt

3 large eggs

1 1/2 cups sugar

1 1/4 cup vegetable oil

2 teaspoons pure vanilla extract

2 cups grated zucchini (2 to 3 medium zucchini)

Preheat the oven to 350°F. Line 24 cupcake tins with baking papers. Sift together the flour, baking soda, ginger, nutmeg, and salt. Set aside.

Beat together the eggs and sugar. Add the oil and vanilla and beat to combine. Stir in the zucchini. Add the flour mixture and stir to combine.

Fill each baking paper two-thirds full. Bake until a skewer inserted into the middle of a cupcake comes out clean, about 20 minutes.

MAKES 24 CUPCAKES

Craving homemade cupcakes but haven't got a lot of time? These only take about 20 minutes hands-on time. The secret to making creamed butter icing delicious is to use good-quality real vanilla extract to cover up the raw taste of the confectioners' sugar. A cupcake this classic and simple calls for the generous use of colored sprinkles.

summer breezes

1   recipe One Bowl Vanilla Cupcakes (page 23)

1   recipe Easy Buttercream (page 40)

Sprinkles

Frost cupcakes, and decorate tops with sprinkles of your choice.

MAKES 24 CUPCAKES

This classic Southern cake combines the bright sweetness of pineapple with the rich nuttiness of coconut, and the headiness of ripe bananas.

hummingbird cupcakes

2$^1/_2$ cups all-purpose flour

1 teaspoon baking soda

1 teaspoon ground cinnamon

$^1/_2$ teaspoon salt

3 large eggs

1$^1/_2$ cups sugar

1 cup vegetable oil

2 cups mashed ripe bananas (about 3 medium bananas)

One 8-ounce can crushed pineapple, drained

1$^1/_4$ cups sweetened coconut flakes

Preheat the oven to 350°F. Line 24 cupcake tins with baking papers. Sift together the flour, baking soda, cinnamon, and salt. Set aside.

Beat together the eggs and sugar. Beat in the oil. Stir in the bananas, pineapple, and coconut. Add the flour mixture and stir to combine.

Fill each baking paper two-thirds full. Bake until a skewer inserted into the middle of a cupcake comes out clean, about 20 minutes.

MAKES 24 CUPCAKES

These moist cakes capture all the flamboyance of a Polynesian cocktail. Lemon cupcakes are moistened with lemon syrup, and filled with tart-but-sweet passion fruit curd. A little shredded coconut in the center of the cupcakes adds an extra burst of coconut flavor.

tiki cupcakes

1 recipe Lemon Cupcakes (page 22)

1 recipe Lemon Syrup (page 51)

1 recipe Passionfruit Curd (page 49)

1 recipe Coconut Buttercream (page 39)

3 cups sweetened coconut flakes

Preheat the oven to 300°F. Set aside $1/2$ cup of the coconut to go inside the cupcakes. Spread the remaining coconut evenly on a cookie sheet. Toast the coconut until golden and fragrant, about 10 minutes. Transfer to a medium bowl and let cool.

Brush the tops of the cupcakes generously with syrup. Insert a paring knife into the center of each cupcake to make a crevice. Tuck a teaspoon of the reserved coconut into each crevice. Fit a pastry bag with a plain #8, #9, or #10 tip and fill with curd. Pipe the curd into the crevices of the cupcakes. Frost each cupcake with the Coconut Buttercream. Dip the tops of the cupcakes into the toasted coconut.

MAKES 24 CUPCAKES

apple cupcakes

4 tart cooking apples, such as Granny Smith, peeled and diced

2 cups sugar

2 cups all-purpose flour

1 teaspoon cinnamon

$1/4$ teaspoon cloves

$1/4$ teaspoon salt

$3/4$ teaspoon baking soda

1 cup vegetable oil

2 eggs

Preheat the oven to 350°F. Line 24 cupcake tins with baking papers. Combine the apples and sugar and let stand for 1 hour.

In a medium bowl, sift together the flour, cinnamon, cloves, salt, and baking soda. In a small bowl, whisk together the oil and eggs. Whisk the egg mixture into the flour mixture. Stir in the apple mixture.

Fill each paper two-thirds full. Bake until a toothpick inserted into the center comes out clean, 18 to 20 minutes.

MAKES 24 CUPCAKES

This is designed to satisfy the tooth of the most ardent lemon-desserts lover. Lemon Buttermilk cupcakes are soaked with a lemon syrup, filled with lemon curd, and then frosted with lemon buttercream. For an easier version, use storebought curd, or leave it out altogether.

lemonade stand

1 recipe Lemon, Orange, or Lime Buttermilk Cupcakes (page 22)

1 recipe Lemon, Orange, or Lime Syrup (page 51)

1 recipe Lemon, Orange, or Lime Curd (pages 48 or 50; optional)

1 recipe Lemon, Orange, or Lime Buttercream (page 39)

Brush the tops of the cupcakes generously with syrup. If filling the cupcakes with curd, insert a paring knife into the center of each cupcake to make a crevice. Fit a pastry bag with a plain round #8, #9, or #10 tip, and fill the bag with curd. Pipe curd into the crevices. Frost the cupcakes with the buttercream.

MAKES 24 CUPCAKES

quick fruit cupcakes

$^1/_2$ cup sugar

$^1/_2$ cup water

$^2/_3$ cup dark rum

2 cups golden raisins

1 cup currants

$1^1/_2$ cups cake flour

$1^1/_2$ teaspoons baking powder

$^1/_2$ teaspoon baking soda

$^1/_2$ teaspoon freshly grated nutmeg

$^1/_2$ teaspoon salt

1 cup (2 sticks) unsalted butter

1 cup packed light-brown sugar

2 large eggs

$^1/_2$ cup milk

$1^1/_2$ cups sweetened coconut flakes

Combine the sugar, water, and rum in a small saucepan. Bring to a boil, reduce to a simmer, and cook until the sugar dissolves, about 4 minutes. Remove from heat, add the raisins and currants, and let stand until the fruit is soft and has absorbed most of the liquid, about 1 hour.

Preheat the oven to 325°F. Line 24 cupcake tins with baking papers. Sift together the flour, baking powder, baking soda, nutmeg, and salt. Set aside.

In the bowl of an electric mixer, cream together the butter and sugar until fluffy, about 3 minutes. Add the eggs, one at a time, beating well after each addition. Alternately add the flour mixture and the milk, beginning and ending with flour. Drain the fruit of any excess liquid, and fold the fruit into the batter. Fold in the coconut.

Fill each paper two-thirds full. Bake until a toothpick inserted into the center comes out clean, 22 to 24 minutes.

MAKES 24 CUPCAKES

25¢

red velvet cupcakes

2$^1/_2$ cups cake flour

2 tablespoons cocoa

1 teaspoon baking soda

$^1/_2$ teaspoon salt

1 cup (2 sticks) unsalted butter, at room temperature

1$^1/_2$ cups sugar

2 teaspoons pure vanilla extract

Red food coloring

2 large eggs

1 cup buttermilk

Preheat the oven to 350°F. Line 24 cupcake tins with baking papers. Sift together the flour, cocoa, baking soda, and salt. Set aside.

In the bowl of an electric mixer, cream together the butter and sugar until fluffy, about 3 minutes. Add the vanilla. Add enough food coloring to turn the mixture a deep red; beat to combine. Add the eggs, one at a time, beating well after each addition. Alternately add flour mixture and buttermilk, beginning and ending with the flour.

Fill each baking paper two-third full. Bake until a skewer inserted into the middle of a cupcake comes out clean, about 20 minutes.

MAKES 24 CUPCAKES

These make a huge impression at childrens' parties. Flat-bottomed wafer cones are filled with a small amount of rich brownie batter, baked, and generously iced with a tall rosette of stabilized whipped cream. If you would rather forego the process of stabilizing whipped cream, pipe cupcakes with Chantilly Cream right before serving.

ice cream cones

1   recipe raw Fudgie Brownie Cupcakes batter (page 36)

1½ recipes plain-flavored or Strawberry Stabilized Cream (page 43; prepare after cones are baked and cooled)

    Sprinkles, jimmies, or nonpareils

24 wafer ice cream cones with flat bottoms

Preheat the oven to 350°F. Place 12 wafer cones on each of two sturdy baking sheets. Fill each cone a half-inch from the top with the fudge brownie batter. Bake until a skewer inserted into the middle of a brownie comes out clean, about 12 minutes. Remove the cones from the oven and let cool.

Fit a large pastry bag with a large #16 star tip. Prepare the stabilized cream, and fill the pastry bag with it. Starting just inside the outer edge of a cupcake, begin piping a swirl of icing. Continue piping in a circular motion, making the swirl narrower each time around, until you have piped a 2-inch high rosette. Repeat with the remaining cones. Scatter sprinkles over the icing.

MAKES 24 CUPCAKES

fudgie brownie cupcakes

Four 1-ounce squares unsweetened baking chocolate

6 tablespoons (³/₄ stick) unsalted butter

1 cup sugar

2 large eggs

²/₃ cup all-purpose flour

¹/₂ teaspoon salt

¹/₂ teaspoon baking powder

Preheat the oven to 375°F. Melt the chocolate and the butter in the top of a double boiler. Remove from heat and whisk in the sugar and eggs. Sift together the flour, salt, and baking powder. Whisk the flour mixture into the chocolate mixture until just combined. Use batter according to cupcake recipe instructions.

MAKES 48 MINI OR 24 MEDIUM CUPCAKES

ice cream cones

basic frostings & fillings

If you decide to forego piping, you can help snackers differentiate between the two flavors of cake by using orange sprinkles on the carrot, and green on the zucchini.

carrot & zucchini cupcakes

$^1/_2$ recipe Carrot Cupcakes (page 30)

$^1/_2$ recipe Zucchini Cupcakes (page 31)

$1^1/_2$ recipes Cream Cheese Icing (page 44)

Orange food coloring

Leaf green food coloring

Transfer 1 cup of the icing to a small bowl. Stir in enough orange food coloring to create a vibrant carrot-orange. Transfer another cup of icing to a small bowl. Stir in enough leaf green food coloring to create the green icing for the squash and carrot leaves. Using an offset spatula, frost each cupcake with the reserved, white icing.

Fit a pastry bag with a plain round #10 tip. Fill with orange icing. Pipe a line in the center of a carrot cupcake, drawing the end of the icing to a point so that it looks like a carrot. Repeat on the remaining carrot cupcakes. Rinse out the pastry bag. Fit with a coupler and a plain #3 pastry tip. Fill with green icing. Pipe three lines coming out of the base of each carrot to resemble carrot greens.

Use the same pastry bag and tip to pipe squash tendrils on the zucchini cupcakes. Pipe a couple curliques coming out of the center of each cupcake. Remove the plain tip and switch to a #68 or #69 leaf tip. Pipe two or three leaf shapes (see page 19) in the center of each zucchini cupcake for the squash leaves.

MAKES 24 CUPCAKES

swiss meringue buttercream

4 large egg whites

1 cup sugar

$1/2$ teaspoon salt

$1/4$ teaspoon cream of tartar

2 cups (4 sticks) unsalted butter, at room temperature, cut into $1/2$-inch pieces

1 teaspoon pure vanilla extract

In the top of a double boiler set over simmering water, whisk together the egg whites, sugar, salt, and cream of tartar. Continue whisking until the mixture becomes too hot to touch comfortably, 7 to 10 minutes.

Transfer the mixture to the bowl of an electric mixer fitted with a whisk attachment. Beat on medium-high speed until the egg whites hold a stiff peak, about 8 minutes. Add the butter, one or two pieces at a time, beating after each addition until incorporated. Beat in the vanilla. Use at room temperature.

MAKES 3 CUPS, ENOUGH TO FROST 24 CUPCAKES

carrot & zucchini cupcakes

buttercream variations

TO MAKE BROWN SUGAR BUTTERCREAM

Follow the instructions for Swiss Meringue Buttercream, substituting 1 cup packed dark brown sugar for the granulated sugar.

TO MAKE PEANUT BUTTER BUTTERCREAM

Follow the instructions for Brown Sugar Buttercream, adding $1/4$ cup creamy peanut butter along with the vanilla.

TO MAKE HONEY BUTTERCREAM

Follow the instructions for Swiss Meringue Buttercream, substituting $3/4$ cup honey for $3/4$ cup of the sugar.

TO MAKE COCONUT BUTTERCREAM

Follow the instructions for Swiss Meringue Buttercream and add either $1/2$ cup sweetened canned coconut cream (such as Coco Lopez), or 3 ounces pure creamed coconut, a dense, highly flavored brick of coconut fat, sometimes found in the international sections of supermarkets. Do not confuse pure creamed coconut with the liquid coconut cream that comes in a can.

TO MAKE LEMON, LIME, OR ORANGE BUTTERCREAM

Follow instructions for Swiss Meringue Buttercream and add 3 tablespoons of either lemon juice, lime juice, or Grand Marnier (for the orange version). Then grate and add the zest of either one lemon, two limes, or one orange. If you don't want to add the zest, substitute either 2 drops of lemon oil, lime oil, or orange oil (available at specialty baking stores). Stir to combine.

Crushed cookies make the sand for these sunshiney cakes. The sand castles are slightly more time-consuming to make than the umbrellas, so if you are pressed for time, you may want to stick with just Beach Umbrella Cupcakes.

sand castles & beach umbrella cupcakes

1	recipe Blueberry Cupcakes (page 29)
1¹/₂	recipes Lemon Cream Cheese Icing (page 44)
4	cups Nilla Wafers or other blonde cookie
2	feet wire-edged ribbon cut into 2-inch lengths
	Thin wooden skewers cut into twelve 3-inch lengths
12	cocktail umbrellas

To make the flags for the sand castles, cut a V out of one edge of each length of ribbon. Fasten the flat side of the uncut end of ribbon to the top of a skewer using a small piece of tape. Repeat with remaining skewers and ribbons.

Frost the tops of 12 cupcakes with Lemon Cream Cheese Icing and set aside. Unwrap the remaining 12 cupcakes, and turn them bottom side up. Using an offset spatula, frost the sides and bottom of each cupcake as evenly as possible with the remaining cream cheese icing. Place all 24 cupcakes bottom side up in the refrigerator so that the icing becomes firm, about 15 minutes.

Meanwhile, grind the wafers into fine crumbs in a food processor. Transfer the crumbs to a medium bowl. Roll the icing-coated tops and sides of the unwrapped cupcakes in the crumbs. Garnish each with a flag. Roll the tops of the wrapped cupcakes in the crumbs. Garnish each with an open cocktail umbrella.

MAKES 24 REGULAR OR 48 MINI CUPCAKES

This is classic American-style icing, very popular at bake sales for the past fifty years. It's a little denser and sweeter than Swiss Meringue Buttercream. It's quick to whip up, and probably the most popular type of icing in this country.

easy buttercream

4 tablespoons unsalted butter, at room temperature

1 one-pound box (about 4 cups) confectioners' sugar

Pinch of salt

1 teaspoon pure vanilla extract

2 to 4 tablespoons milk

Using a hand-held electric mixer or a standing mixer fitted with a paddle attachment, cream the butter until fluffy, about 2 minutes. On low speed, gradually beat in the confectioners' sugar. Add the salt and vanilla. Beat in 2 tablespoons of the milk, adding more milk if needed to reach spreading consistency. Cover the surface of the icing with plastic wrap until you're ready to frost the cupcakes.

MAKES 2^1/$_2$ CUPS, ENOUGH TO FROST 24 CUPCAKES

easy chocolate buttercream

Three 1-ounce squares unsweetened chocolate, roughly chopped

4   tablespoons unsalted butter, at room temperature

1   one-pound box (about 4 cups) confectioners' sugar

Pinch of salt

1   teaspoon pure vanilla extract

4 to 6   tablespoons milk

Place the chocolate in the top of a gently simmering double boiler.
Stir occasionally until melted, about 6 minutes. Using a hand-held electric
mixer or a standing mixer fitted with a paddle attachment, cream the
butter until fluffy, about 2 minutes. Add the melted chocolate and beat to
combine. On low speed, gradually beat in the confectioners' sugar.
Add the salt and vanilla. Beat in 4 tablespoons of the milk, adding more
milk if needed to reach spreading consistency. Cover the surface of
the icing with plastic wrap until you're ready to frost the cupcakes.

MAKES 2$^{1}/_{2}$ CUPS, ENOUGH TO FROST 24 CUPCAKES

summer

This recipe contains raw egg whites. If you or your guests suffer from a weak immune system, substitute meringue powder and water to avoid any possibility of infection. Meringue powder can be found at specialty baking supply stores, or ordered online.

almond sugar glaze

1 one-pound box (about 4 cups) confectioners' sugar

2 large very fresh egg whites, or 5 tablespoons meringue powder combined with $1/3$ cup water

$1/2$ to $3/4$ cup water

$1/4$ teaspoon almond extract

$1/4$ teaspoon orange oil

In the bowl of an electric mixer fitted with a paddle attachment, combine the confectioners' sugar with the egg whites or meringue powder and water. Beat until the mixture is thick and fluffy, about 5 minutes. On low speed, begin adding the water gradually. Stop mixing when the icing holds a ribbon dropped from a spoon for 7 seconds. Stir in the almond extract and orange oil.

MAKES $2^{1}/_{3}$ CUPS, ENOUGH TO COAT 24 CUPCAKES

These moist jam cupcakes are deliciously complemented by swirls of stabilized whipped cream. Plain cream cheese icing also provides a similar creamy contrast.

strawberries & cream

1 recipe Jam Cupcakes (page 28)

1 recipe Stabilized Whipped Cream or Cream Cheese Icing (pages 43 or 44)

2 cups seedless raspberry, strawberry, or blackberry jam

Insert a paring knife into the center of each cupcake to make a crevice. Fit a pastry bag with a plain round #8, #9, or #10 tip, and fill the bag with jam. Pipe jam into the crevices of the cupcakes. Frost each cupcake with the whipped cream.

MAKES 24 CUPCAKES

chantilly cream

2 cups heavy cream, chilled

3 to 4 teaspoons confectioners' sugar

2 teaspoons pure vanilla extract

Place the heavy cream in a chilled mixing bowl or the chilled bowl of a standing mixer. Using a hand-held mixer or a standing mixer fitted with a whisk attachment, beat on medium speed until the cream is almost doubled in volume and holds a soft peak.

MAKES 3 3/4 CUPS, ENOUGH TO TOP 24 CUPCAKES

easy variations

TO MAKE STABILIZED WHIPPED CREAM

Follow the instructions for Chantilly Cream, but do not beat all the way. Place 2 tablespoons cold water in a small heatproof mixing bowl. Sprinkle 2 teaspoons gelatin over the water. Let sit until the gelatin has expanded, softened, and absorbed all the water, about 10 minutes. Place the bowl over a small saucepan of gently simmering water. Stir the gelatin constantly until dissolved, about 6 minutes. Whisk 1/4 cup of the half-beaten cream into the liquid gelatin. Continue beating the cream while adding the gelatin mixture in a stream. Beat until the cream holds a soft peak.

TO MAKE STRAWBERRY STABILIZED CREAM

Follow the instructions for Stabilized Whipped Cream, adding 1/3 cup seedless strawberry jelly to the gelatin mixture instead of 1/4 cup half-beaten cream.

The frilly piping on these cupcakes resembles the ruffles of a Spanish dancer's skirt. To create extra-flamboyant striated ruffles, fill your pastry bag with two different tones of buttercream.

cinqo de mayo fiesta cupcakes

1   recipe Coconut Cupcakes (page 27)
1   recipe Easy Buttercream (page 40)
    Orange food coloring
    Colored sprinkles or jimmies

Transfer 1 cup of the buttercream to a medium bowl. Add enough orange food coloring to create a rich color. Fit a pastry bag with a plain basket or petal tip such as a #45 or #150. Smear some orange buttercream on one side of the inside of the pastry bag. Fill the rest of the bag with white buttercream.

Starting at the outer edge of a cupcake, pipe a frilly edge onto the cupcake by drawing the pastry tip back and forth in a wavy motion. Continue spiraling the frill of icing toward the center of the cupcake until the entire surface of the cupcake is covered in loose frills. Repeat with the remaining cupcakes. Scatter sprinkles over the tops of the cupcakes to look like confetti.

MAKES 24 CUPCAKES

cream cheese icing

8 ounces cream cheese, at room temperature

$^1/_2$ cup (1 stick) unsalted butter

$1^1/_2$ teaspoons pure vanilla extract

1 one-pound box (about 4 cups) confectioners' sugar, sifted

Using a hand-held electric mixer or a standing mixer fitted with a paddle attachment, beat the cream cheese and butter until fluffy, about 2 minutes. Beat in the vanilla. On low speed, gradually add the confectioners' sugar, beating until combined. Cover the surface of the icing with plastic wrap until you're ready to frost the cupcakes.

MAKES $2^1/_2$ CUPS, ENOUGH TO FROST 24 CUPCAKES

flavor variations

TO MAKE LEMON CREAM CHEESE ICING

Follow the instructions for Cream Cheese Icing, stirring in the finely grated zest of one lemon.

TO MAKE MALTED MILK ICING

Follow the instructions for Cream Cheese Icing, stirring in 1 cup malted milk powder, such as Horlick's.

If making these ahead of time, use Stabilized Whipped Cream, or you can add the Chantilly Cream at the last minute.

black forest cherry cupcakes

1 recipe Chocolate Sour Cream Cupcakes (page 25)

1 recipe Chantilly Cream or Stabilized Whipped Cream (page 43)

8 cups cherries, pitted

1/2 cup kirsch, plus 1 tablespoon for the Chantilly Cream

1/4 cup confectioners' sugar, for sifting (optional)

Place the cherries and 1/2 cup kirsch in a medium saucepan. Bring the kirsch to a boil and let simmer over medium heat until the cherries begin to soften, about 6 minutes. Set aside to cool. Fold the remaining kirsch into the Chantilly Cream.

Using a paring knife, cut a cone from the top of each cupcake and set them aside. Brush the inside of each cupcake with a little of the cherry syrup from the cooked cherries. Fill each cupcake with a couple of softened cherries, and top each one with a dollop of Chantilly Cream. If desired, drizzle a little more cherry syrup over the whipped cream.

Place the reserved cones of cupcake on top of the whipped cream to form lids. Sift the powdered sugar over the cupcakes.

MAKES 24 CUPCAKES

Booklets containing 25 leaves of edible gold are available at specialty baking stores. Because the gold has to be very pure to be edible it's quite pricey. If you want to make your gold leaf last, try doing one sheet pan of Fallen Leaves with gold leaf and one without. The effect of the gold is well worth the expense and perfect for special occasions.

fallen leaves

1 1/2 teaspoons olive oil, plus more for oiling baking sheets

9 to 18 leaves of edible gold leaf (optional)

1 pound good-quality semisweet chocolate (such as Valrhona), chopped

If using gold leaf, rub the surface of two 11-by-17-inch baking sheets with an oiled paper towel. Hold the booklet of gold leaf in your hand and peel back one square of paper to reveal a square of gold leaf. Gently invert the booklet onto the pan so that the sheet of gold sticks to the oiled surface of the pan. Repeat the process with 8 more gold squares, spacing them out evenly. Adhere 9 more gold squares to the other baking sheet.

Place chocolate and olive oil in a medium heatproof bowl. Set bowl over a saucepan of gently simmering water. Using a rubber spatula or whisk, stir occasionally until chocolate is just melted. Pour half of chocolate into each baking sheet. Using an offset spatula spread chocolate evenly from edge to edge of each pan. Place pans in the refrigerator to harden, about 15 minutes. Break hardened sheet of chocolate into 1-to-3-inch shards. Keep shards in the refrigerator until ready to decorate cupcakes.

MAKES ENOUGH TO DECORATE 24 CUPCAKES

black forest cherry cupcakes

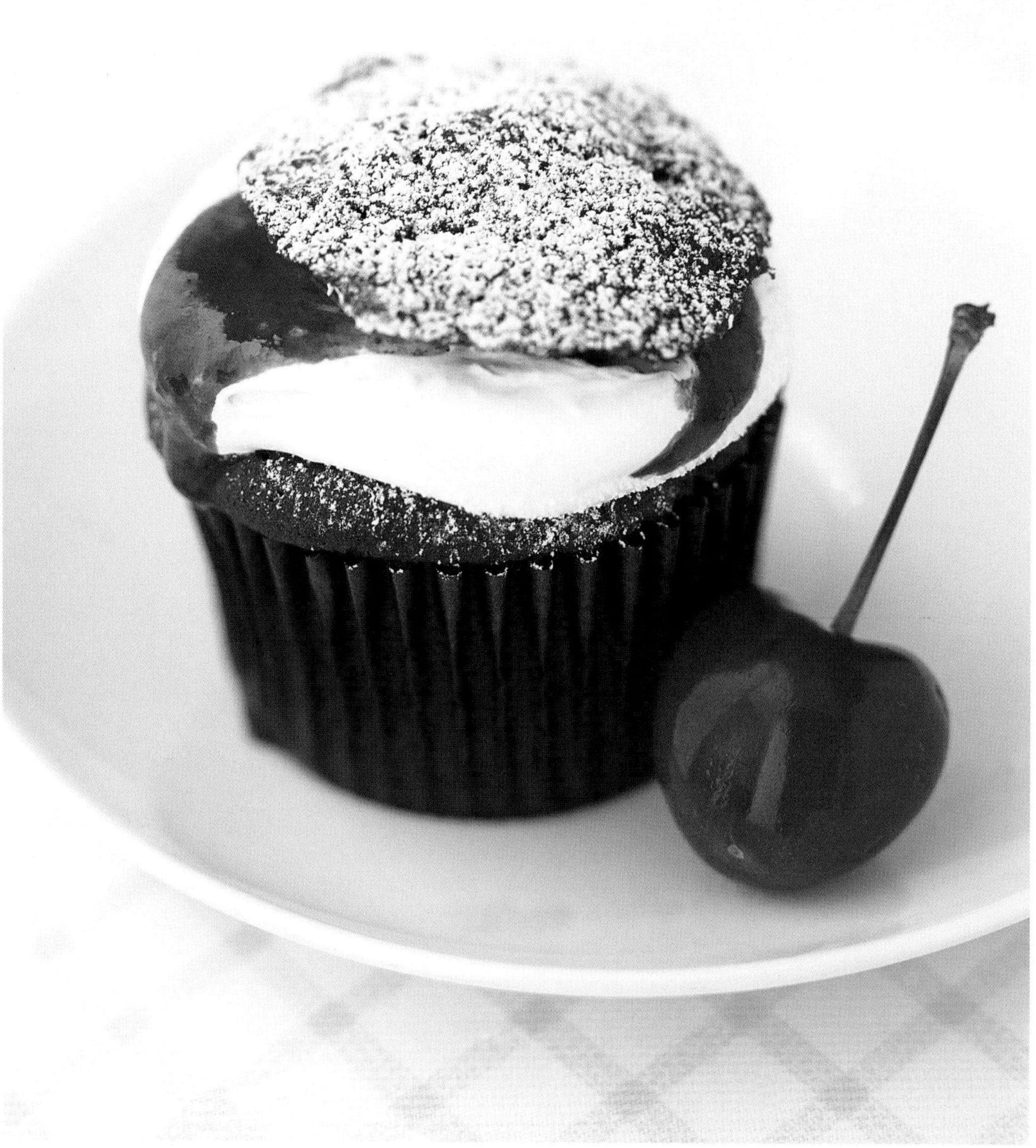

caramel icing

2 cups packed light brown sugar

1 cup heavy cream

1/4 teaspoon salt

2 tablespoons light corn syrup

6 tablespoons (3/4 stick) unsalted butter, cut into 6 pieces

Place the brown sugar, cream, salt, and corn syrup in a heavy-bottomed saucepan. Bring to a boil over medium-high heat. Continue to cook until the mixture reaches 240°F on a candy thermometer. Remove from heat and let cool to 110°F. Beat in the butter, one piece at a time, until all the butter is combined and the mixture is almost room temperature. Use immediately.

MAKES 3 CUPS, ENOUGH TO FROST 24 CUPCAKES

white chocolate for piping

1 cup white chocolate, either in chips or chopped

1/3 cup heavy cream

Place the chocolate in the top of a gently simmering double boiler. Stir occasionally until the chocolate is melted, about 8 minutes. Add the cream. Be sure to keep the water at a very gentle simmer, or the chocolate mixture may curdle. Use while still warm.

MAKES 1 CUP, ENOUGH TO DECORATE 24 CUPCAKES

These are an easy alternative to petits fours. Rather than worrying about painstakingly glazing whole little cakes, leave miniature cupcakes in their frilly wrappers and just glaze the tops. The hard sugar glaze also serves to keep the cakes moist and fresh. Sliced almonds imitate a butterfly alighting on the top of each.

pastel petit fours

1 recipe Browned Butter Nut Cupcakes (page 26)

1 recipe Almond Sugar Glaze (page 42)

Lemon yellow, leaf green, and sky blue food coloring

96 sliced almonds (2 per cupcake)

Divide the glaze between three small bowls. Add a small amount of food coloring to each of the bowls so you have three different colors of glaze. Ice the cupcakes by evenly spreading 2 teaspoons glaze over each. You will have eight cupcakes each color. Let the cupcakes sit until the glaze hardens slightly, about 20 minutes.

Select two pieces of sliced almonds that are approximately the same size. Place them wide side down at an angle to each other on the top of a cake to create a butterfly. Repeat with the remaining cupcakes.

MAKES 48 MINI CUPCAKES

chocolate glaze

12 ounces semisweet chocolate, either in chips or chopped

1 1/2 cups heavy cream

Place the chocolate and cream in the top of a gently simmering double boiler. Stir occasionally until the chocolate is melted, about 10 minutes. Remove from heat. Use while still warm and liquid. If the glaze becomes too thick to work with, reheat it.

MAKES 2 2/3 CUPS, ENOUGH TO COAT 24 CUPCAKES

whipped chocolate ganache

Follow the instructions for Chocolate Glaze, but transfer the warm glaze to a bowl and place in the refrigerator to chill. Stir occasionally until the glaze has cooled and thickened to the consistency of sour cream, about 1 hour. Using a hand-held electric mixer or a standing mixer, beat on medium speed until the ganache is fluffy, thick, and lighter in color, about 5 minutes.

MAKES 3 1/2 CUPS

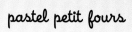

Homemade curd will keep in the refrigerator up to one week, and will keep frozen for up to three months.

lemon curd

1/3 cup lemon juice

1 tablespoon cornstarch

1 cup sugar

Grated zest of 2 lemons

6 egg yolks

1/2 cup (1 stick) cold unsalted butter, cut into 1/2-inch pieces

In the top of a double boiler, whisk together the lemon juice and corn-starch. Add the sugar, zest, and egg yolks; whisk to combine.

Bring the water in the double boiler to a simmer. Using a whisk, stir the mixture until thick enough to coat the back of a wooden spoon, about 20 minutes. Whisk in the butter, one or two pieces at a time. When all the butter is combined, transfer the curd to a clean bowl. Cover the surface of the curd with plastic wrap and place in the refrigerator to cool.

MAKES 2 CUPS, ENOUGH TO FILL 24 CUPCAKES

Marshmallow Peeps only come around once a year, so why not make the most of them? You may have to trim a little off the bottom of your bunny to get him to stand upright.

bunny cupcakes

 1 recipe Buttermilk Cupcakes (page 22)
 1 recipe Swiss Meringue Buttercream (page 38), tinted leaf green
24 bunny-shaped Peeps
 4 feet narrow ribbon for bunnies' bow ties (optional)

Using an offset spatula, frost each cupcake with the buttercream, reserving ²/₃ cup for piping the leaves. If desired, tie a 2-inch length of ribbon around each of the bunnies' necks to form a bow tie. Trim the ends of the ribbon to desired length.

Place a Peeps bunny in the center of each cupcake. Fit a pastry bag with a #366 or #67 leaf tip. Fill the bag with the reserved buttercream. Pipe small leaves around the base of each bunny.

MAKES 24 CUPCAKES

Passion fruit juices are available as bottled or boxed nectars, or frozen concentrate. If using the concentrate it is not necessary to reduce it over the stove. Merely substitute $^1/_2$ cup thawed concentrate.

passionfruit curd

2 cups passionfruit nectar

1 cup sugar

6 egg yolks

$^1/_2$ cup (1 stick) cold unsalted butter, cut into $^1/_2$ inch pieces

Place the passion fruit nectar in a small saucepan and bring to a boil over medium-high heat. Let simmer until reduced to $^1/_2$ cup. Transfer the mixture to the top of a double boiler. Add the sugar and egg yolks; whisk to combine.

Bring the bottom of the double boiler to a simmer. Using a whisk, stir the mixture until thick enough to coat the back of a wooden spoon, about 20 minutes. Whisk in the butter, one or two pieces at a time. When all the butter is combined, transfer the curd to a clean bowl. Cover the surface of the curd with plastic wrap and place in the refrigerator to cool.

MAKES 2 CUPS, ENOUGH TO FILL 24 CUPCAKES

These easy cupcakes take no skill to decorate, but get a strong reaction from little kids. Nests can be filled with whatever round Easter candies you have on hand.

easter egg nests

1   recipe Buttermilk Cupcakes (page 22)

1   recipe Swiss Meringue Buttercream, Brown Sugar Buttercream, or Easy Buttercream (page 38, 39, or 40)

2   cups sweetened coconut flakes

72 candy-coated Jordan almonds or unwrapped chocolate Easter eggs (3 per cupcake)

Preheat the oven to 300°F. Spread the coconut evenly on a cookie sheet. Toast the coconut until golden and fragrant, about 10 minutes. Transfer to a medium bowl and let cool.

Using an offset spatula, frost each cupcake with the buttercream. Roll the top of each cupcake in the toasted coconut to form a nest. Snuggle three Jordan almonds or three chocolate eggs into the center of each nest.

MAKES 24 CUPCAKES

orange curd

1 1/2 cups orange juice

1 cup sugar

Grated zest of two oranges

6 egg yolks

1/2 cup (1 stick) cold unsalted butter, cut into 1/2-inch pieces

Place the orange juice in a small saucepan and bring to a boil over medium-high heat. Let it simmer until reduced to 1/2 cup. Transfer the mixture to the top of a double boiler. Add the sugar, zest, and egg yolks; whisk to combine. Bring the bottom of the double boiler to a simmer. Using a whisk, stir the mixture until thick enough to coat the back of a wooden spoon, about 20 minutes. Whisk in the butter, one or two pieces at a time. When all the butter is combined, transfer the curd to a clean bowl. Cover the surface of the curd with plastic wrap, and place in the refrigerator to cool.

MAKES 2 CUPS, ENOUGH TO FILL 24 CUPCAKES

lime curd

1/3 cup lime juice

1 tablespoon cornstarch

1 cup sugar

Grated zest of 3 limes

6 egg yolks

1/2 cup (1 stick) cold unsalted butter, cut into 1/2-inch pieces

In the top of a double boiler, whisk together the lime juice and cornstarch. Add the sugar, zest, and egg yolks; whisk to combine. Bring the bottom of the double boiler to a simmer. Using a whisk, stir the mixture until it's thick enough to coat the back of a wooden spoon, about 20 minutes. Whisk in the butter, one or two pieces at a time. When all the butter is combined, transfer the curd to a clean bowl. Cover the surface of the curd with plastic wrap and place in the refrigerator to cool.

MAKES 2 CUPS, ENOUGH TO FILL 24 CUPCAKES

bunny cupcakes & easter egg nests

lemon syrup

1	cup sugar	Finely grated zest of 1 lemon
1	cup water	Juice of 1 lemon, strained

Combine the sugar and water in a small saucepan. Bring to a boil. Reduce to a simmer and add the zest and juice. Cook until slightly thickened, about 10 minutes. The syrup will keep for up to 2 weeks if refrigerated in an airtight container.

MAKES 1 1/3 CUPS, ENOUGH TO TOP 24 CUPCAKES

flavor variations

TO MAKE ORANGE SYRUP

Follow the instructions for Lemon Syrup, substituting orange zest for the lemon zest and orange juice for the lemon juice.

TO MAKE LIME SYRUP

Follow the instructions for Lemon Syrup, substituting lime zest for the lemon zest and lime juice for the lemon juice.

TO MAKE BRANDY OR RUM SYRUP

Follow the instructions for Lemon Syrup, substituting 3 tablespoons good-quality brandy or rum for the lemon juice and lemon zest.

TO MAKE ESPRESSO SYRUP

Follow the instructions for Lemon Syrup, substituting 1/4 cup strong espresso for the lemon juice and lemon zest. If you don't have an espresso maker, combine 3 tablespoons water with 2 tablespoons instant espresso powder.

This simple hibiscus flower is a good way to dress up any cupcake. You'll find that the Swiss Meringue Buttercream lends itself to piping the best, although once you have the knack Cream Cheese Icing works very well too. Practice piping the flower on the surface of a cutting board until you feel comfortable.You can always scrape up the piped icing and place it back in the pastry bag.

blossom cupcakes

1   recipe Buttermilk Cupcakes (page 22)

1   and one-half recipes Swiss Meringue Buttercream (page 38),
    room temperature

    Food coloring

2   tablespoons yellow jimmies or round colored candies

Transfer 2 cups of the buttercream to a medium bowl, and use food coloring to tint the buttercream to the color of your choice. Using an offset spatula, frost the cupcakes with the reserved white buttercream. Fit a pastry bag with a #104 petal tip. Fill the bag with the tinted buttercream. Follow instructions for piping the flower on page 19.

MAKES 24 CUPCAKES

honey lemon syrup

1 cup honey

1/2 cup water

Finely grated zest of one lemon

Juice of one lemon, strained

Combine the honey and water in a small saucepan. Bring to a boil over medium-high heat. Reduce to a simmer and continue to cook until slightly thickened, about 5 minutes.

MAKES 1 1/2 CUPS, ENOUGH TO COAT 24 CUPCAKES

blossom cupcakes

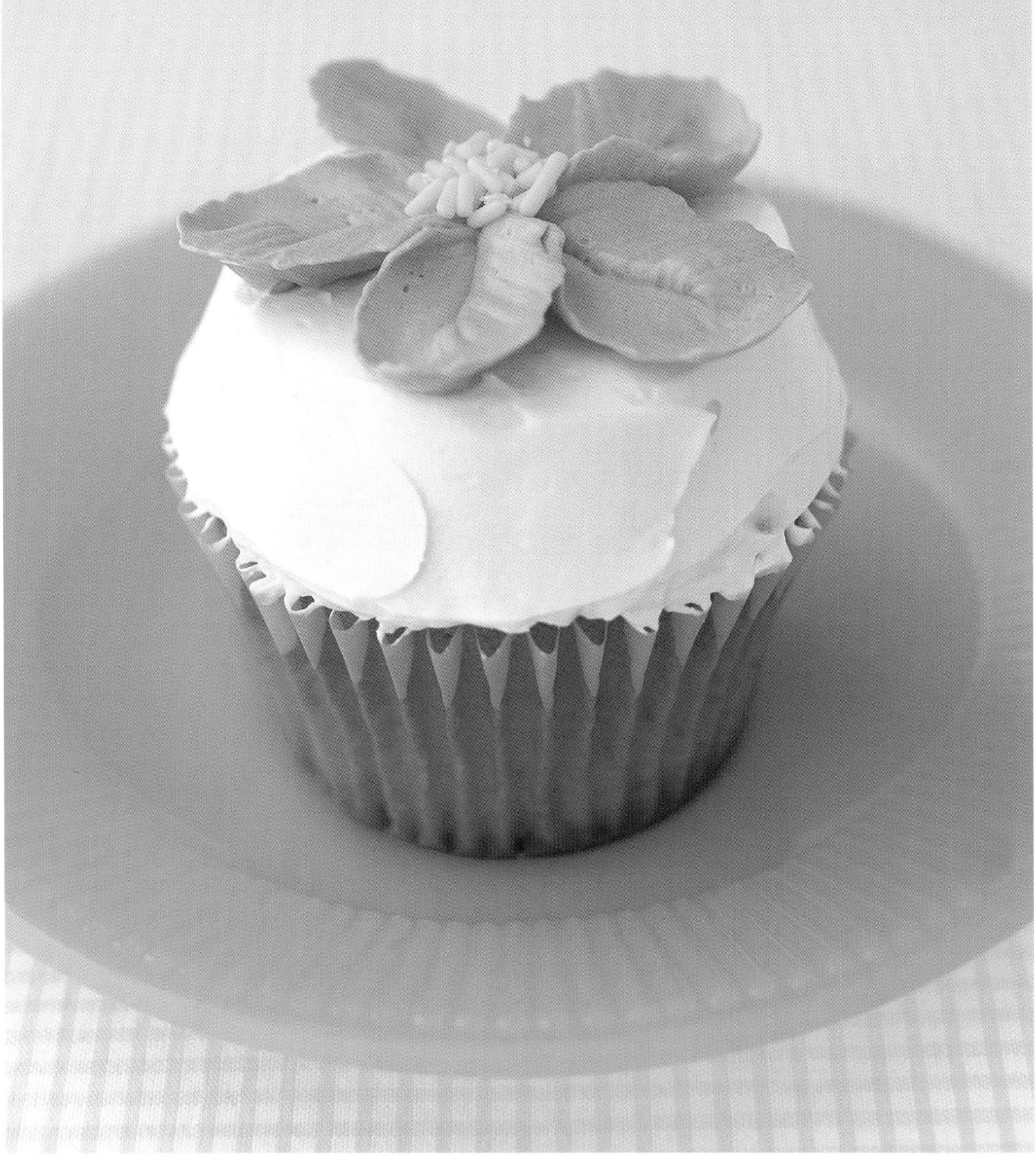

cinnamon streusel

- 1   cup all-purpose flour
- 1   cup light brown sugar
- 8   tablespoons (1 stick) unsalted butter, melted
- 1$\frac{1}{2}$ teaspoons ground cinnamon
- 1   cup walnuts, chopped

In a medium bowl, combine flour, sugar, butter, and cinnamon with a fork. Stir in walnuts.

MAKES 2 CUPS

maple walnut topping

- 3   cups walnut pieces
- 3   cups confectioners' sugar, sifted
- $\frac{1}{3}$ to $\frac{1}{2}$ cup real maple syrup
- 2   teaspoons pure vanilla extract

Preheat the oven to 350°F. Spread the walnuts on a baking sheet. Bake until the walnuts are fragrant and slightly toasted, about 8 minutes. Place the confectioners' sugar in a medium-sized bowl. Whisk in $\frac{1}{3}$ cup maple syrup, adding more maple syrup until the mixture is the consistency of heavy cream. Stir in the vanilla and walnuts. Cover the surface of the topping with plastic wrap until ready to use.

MAKES 4 CUPS, ENOUGH FOR 24 CUPCAKES

spring